Waiting for the Dead to Speak

Other Books by Brian Fanelli

Frontman (Chapbook, Big Table Publishing, 2010)
All That Remains (Unbound Content, LLC, 2013)

Waiting for the Dead to Speak

A Collection of Poems

Brian Fanelli

NYQ Books™

The New York Quarterly Foundation, Inc.
New York, New York

NYQ Books™ is an imprint of The New York Quarterly Foundation, Inc.

The New York Quarterly Foundation, Inc.
P. O. Box 2015
Old Chelsea Station
New York, NY 10113

www.nyq.org

First Edition

Set in New Baskerville

Layout by Raymond P. Hammond

Cover Design by Raymond P. Hammond

Cover Art by Mikayla Lewis

Author Photo by Daryl Sznyter

Library of Congress Control Number: 2016931047

ISBN: 978-1-63045-025-0

Waiting for the Dead to Speak

Acknowledgements

Some of the poems in this book have been published by *The Adirondack Review, Blue Collar Review, Boston Literary Magazine, The Broken Plate, Chiron Review, CityLitRag, Contemporary American Voices, Cooper Street Journal, East Meets West: American Writers Review, Fledgling Rag, Foliate Oak, Ishka Bibble, LABOR, The Lascaux Review, Main Street Rag, Museum of Americana, Oklahoma Review, The Paterson Literary Review, Poetry Quarterly, Popshot, San Pedro River Review, SLAB, Slipstream, Two Cities Review,* and *World Literature Today.*

I would like to express my sincere gratitude to my family and friends and to my colleagues at Lackawanna College. Many thanks to Maria Mazziotti Gillan, Jaimee Wriston Colbert, Joe Weil, Fred Gardaphé, Dawn Leas, Amanda J. Bradley, and Raymond Hammond for their feedback on this book. None of these poems would be possible without all of you and the support of the broader writing community.

Contents

III

This book is dedicated to my teachers, past and present.

I

For Jimmy, Who Bruised My Ribs and Busted My Nose

In our neighborhood, Fat Jimmy descended the mountain,
his chest heaving like a bull,
ready to maul a matador.

He cracked his scarred knuckles, hunted scrawny prey,
curb stomped our basketballs
like heads he wanted to bash,

or ghost rode our bikes
down the garbage trail dump,
until one day I gripped my handlebars

like a soldier clinging to a rifle,
refusing defeat as Jimmy knocked me to my back,
clocked me in the chin.

Numbed, I laughed as he pounded and pounded,
until my nose gushed, my ribs throbbed,
my skin swelled faster than his heated cheeks.

This poem is for the bully who never cried,
who hid belt lashes from us, who ran from the sound
of his father's battered Ford tracking him down,

the son whose hands tightened to fists like his father's,
who uncurled his fingers to study my blood,
and then extended a hand to lift me up.

R.F. Post

In the cool dusk of autumn,
after we retired our bats and gloves,
we biked to R.F. Post,
investigated what lurked behind cracked windows,
what caused the rising stink
near the old post office's cellar doors.
Tony, our town's biggest talker,
whispered rumors of cults,
devil worshippers that spilled blood.
We challenged each other's manhood
with dares to climb the crumbling cement stairs,
touch the rusty doorknob.
Fat Mikey talked big, promised in school
he'd step inside, dispel myths,
quell our curiosity, but he never
came through, just dashed home,
his skin ice-white after we nudged him forward,
or he heard rats and squirrels rustle in shadows.
Two summers later, R.F. Post burned down,
leaving a scorched lot that still smoldered
with rumors of what we imagined lived
behind that paint-peeled door.

Boyhood Summers

We were still boys then when we played capture the flag,
smeared Army Keith's camo make-up on our cheeks,
and then hid in bushes, waiting to point plastic guns
at enemies. We laughed when Bobby
cowered on the ground each time he was shot
and gurgled and gasped, though blood
was spurting from his mouth and nose.

We were just boys then, used to shooter video games
and watching heads explode into pink globs of brain
on the small screen, while our scores
climbed higher and higher with each kill,
just like capture the flag, when we roamed the woods,
stalking the other team, eager to brag
about our casualties at the camp fire
where we ate stale bread and dry fruit
from Army Keith's camo rut sack.

This was years before another war in Iraq,
or ground troops in Afghanistan, years before
Army Keith's marine father had to ship out to combat zones.
We were still boys, unexposed to headlines
about smart bombs and drone strikes.
We were just boys when Bobby smeared fake blood on his cheek,
while we danced around his body, and clenched the flag,
waving it in the air, roaring and hooting,
years before we became familiar with images of burning rubble
and the way real blood darkens to a maroon color and hardens
on the faces of the dead.

What I Imagine My Parents Did After Dinner

In our house, nobody ever danced,
even though my father played Elvis
or Johnny Cash from the silver
CD player that rested on the nook,
separating the kitchen from the dining room.
He could have used the wooden pasta spoon
like a mic and lip-synched along to the King
or the man-in-black, but he just labored
over the stove, his white apron hiding the same
Packers shirt he wore each Sunday,
while the football game blared in the living room,
his mood dependent upon who was winning.

My mother, too, followed routines,
her task to knead the dough,
until flour powdered her hands
and streaked her cheeks,
after she spent hours leaning over the table,
rolling macaroni through the machine.

I like to think that after we ate
two servings of pasta and meatballs,
a salad on the side,
after I helped them scrub pots and pans,
after they untied and washed the aprons,
and I closed my bedroom door to study
or practice guitar scales,
they put on the King or Johnny Cash again
and passed the pasta spoon back and forth
like a karaoke mic and danced around the kitchen,
while moonlight sliced through foliage
and spilled into the kitchen.

Uncanny X-men Issues 141 and 142

When I read *X-men: Days of Future Past,*
I clenched my covers, flipped through pages,
horror-struck that the team of superheroes died,
wiped out in a dystopian future by sentinels
that stalked alleyways, patrolled streets,
busted hideouts where the X-men made a last stand
against a robot army created by man
to destroy mutants because they were different.

When I read issues 141 and 142,
I wept when Storm was impaled,
Colossus was crushed, and even Wolverine
was pulverized by a sentinel's laser blast,
reduced to skeleton.

For months I locked windows, bolted doors,
feared one of those robots would tower in my yard,
yank my family from our home late at night,
jail us in mutant concentration camps.

Now, when I circle the park near my house,
overhear a bully drop the word fag,
or recall the graffitied swastika scrubbed off
a nearby building, I remember how the sentinel's creators
spewed the word mutie again and again in speeches.

At least when I read the final pages,
I could go to sleep knowing
Kitty Pryde succeeded in going back in time
and preventing that awful future.
At least in comics there's a way to revive
superheroes and stop bigots from imprisoning
or exterminating anyone different.

Building the Haunt

By August, I dragged boxes from the attic,
coughed from the dust on crows' wings,
untangled skeletons from cotton cobwebs
and planned how to make my home
a spookhouse throughout October.

By late September I crowded the lawn
with wooden graves, painted names
and dates of the departed—
Doug M. Upp, Seymour Spirits, Willy Rott.

By October, I spun webs around the porch,
placed a red-eyed tarantula in the center,
surrounded by a dozen fake limbs,
splattered with blood.

On the porch, a Frankenstein dummy
watched the neighborhood with battery-operated eyes
and a motion detector mouth that moaned
at anyone who passed.

I wanted to be the boy whose home
earned a front page photo and caption in the paper,
the boy known for more than having his head slammed
into lockers at school and his shots blocked during gym.

I wanted Timmy, Davey and others
who called me pussy to enter the haunt,
and then flee toward the exit when neighborhood kids
I paid in nickels chased them with plastic axes.

I wanted Fat Jimmy, who pummeled me in fifth grade,
to cower behind my pool when I jumped out
in a Michael Myers mask and pretended to strangle
my childhood friend Kevin, who perfected a gasp.

I imagined the spectacle would be enough to earn
high-fives in hallways from Davey, Timmy and all the boys
who pounded me in gym class, who paled at my props
and fled before finishing the haunt.

After Watching *The X-Files*

At ten, I slept on the couch for weeks,
turned the TV low, watched images
flash late into the night, and listened to infomercials
for company and comfort after I spooked myself
watching an *X-Files* episode
about an alien abductee returned to his home.
In the opening shot, he stood in a field,
his arms stiff, his fingers and lips blue,
his skin as pale as a hospital patient's.
My dad never jumped when we watched the creep show
every Sunday at primetime. When he went to bed,
I pondered if aliens could invade my bedroom,
unlock doors and windows,
and then return me after months of experiments.
For weeks I muttered "Hail Mary,"
"Our Father," whatever payers I learned in Sunday school,
while I gripped the silver necklace I wore like a protective charm
against evil spirits and aliens,
knowing that if I caught a glimpse of the supernatural,
or heard a late night creak,
I'd cower under covers, unwilling to confront it
like Mulder and Scully, unwilling to pull back the sheets,
step outside and stare into the night,
brave enough for a moment to confront creatures
I was certain lurked outside.

Halloween

In high school, we crammed into Justin's Chevy,
drove to a no-named road, turned off headlights,
blared the stereo, moshed to The Clash and Minor Threat.
We curled our hands into fists, pretended to scream into a mic,
while our bodies bumped and crashed against each other
and October leaves crunched beneath our Chucks.
We devoured candy bars, until our teeth and lips blackened,
and when we tired, we wiped sweat from our shaggy hair,
panted on the Chevy's blue hood, muted
power chords, and instead played *The Exorcist* theme song.
We gazed at the abandoned farmhouse down the road,
its shingles loose, its porch rotted.
Like neighborhood boys placing bets,
we dared each other to smash windows
where tattered curtains billowed from mid-autumn winds.
I imagined scenes from *The Exorcist,* a demon with decaying flesh
spider walking up and down a cobwebbed staircase.
My friends labeled it a druggie hangout.
They cook meth in there, Justin said.
I saw heroin needles on the lawn last time, Matt added.
We kept our distance, blasted punk rock from the stereo,
forgetting we had no costumes,
we didn't get invited to the party
with six packs and girlfriends willing to investigate
the farmhouse down the road with us.
Instead, we piled kindling, sparked a fire,
danced and slammed beneath a pale moon,
while flames illuminated our jack-o-lantern grins.

Fronting the Band

I always wanted to be the boy
who grew up to front the band,
my fingers forming chords on a Fender Strat,
electricity humming from guitar to amp,
extra picks stuffed in pockets
to give to pleading fans post-show.

Instead, I hung in back,
bobbed my head to bar bands,
Springsteen covers, or the Boss himself,
whose tour buses swallowed half blocks,
whose fans clapped, stomped, screamed,
though hearing gospel,
the bursts of Clarence's sax, the rasp
of Bruce's voice powerful enough
that some passed out stage-front.

At seventeen I formed my own band, Booze Julie,
re-tuned my pawn shop, knock-off Gibson
after every song. We rotated singers,
first Heather who sang too high,
and then Kate who never showed,
until we split, citing creative differences.

Most nights I cranked Bruce, air guitared *Born to Run,*
wiggled and danced in front of mirrors, mimicking
the Boss's manic stage moves, imagining
my band's name printed on t-shirts,
the roar of our guitars, the pulse of our drums
great enough to earn encore after encore, city after city.

Immigrant Names

At ten, when I tanned in summer,
neighborhood boys said I looked Mexican,
my hair dark and shaggy,
my skin brown like dirt they spit upon.

I took no offence, but laughed
when their freckled Irish skin
burned on the baseball mound,
or they had to wear shirts while swimming.

When they rubbed globs of Aloe on redness,
I whispered private thank yous to my grandparents—
Italian immigrants who passed on
their genes and complexions to me.

I didn't know then what it meant
to be othered, the darker friend.
Now I imagine those guys grown, graying,
and wonder if their lips upturn in a sneer

over immigration reform, that same sneer they flashed
when I struck out and they hollered, *Nice play, greaseball,*
forgetting that their great grandparents were called micks
and black and blued because of their freckles and foreign accents.

Looking back I wish I had kicked my cleats on that baseball mound,
clenched my bat, refused to retreat to bleachers,
until I was given a second chance at bat, opportunity to knock the ball
over the fence and slide into home, like any other American boy.

My father never carried a briefcase

never wore a suit with cufflinks
polished to gleam like shoes of lawyers or doctors.
He did wear white dress shirts, loosened top buttons
after work, the weight of his footsteps heavy enough
to make floorboards sigh.
Some days he scooped me in his arms,
until my world blurred,
until I dizzied and laughed.
Other days he yanked off the tie,
said nothing, even at dinner.
I never asked what he did,
only knew he clocked in at an army depot,
his Ford gone before dawn caressed my face,
the hours grinding enough that each night
he dozed on the couch, remote resting
on his belly, rising, falling with each breath.
Before he blared Chuck Norris westerns, I begged
to play catch, and sometimes, he complied,
despite muscle throbs and headaches,
despite the way a son notices
wisps of gray in his father's hair.

Mr. Dobson

We called him Mr. Magoo
when his geezer wagon wobbled into the parking lot.
We slouched at our desks, yawned away his lectures
about European kings and queens from ages
where everyone dressed funny to us.
If we flicked paper footballs, or laughed
at ink blots on his shirts, chalk streaks on his pants,
he halted the lesson, hissed, *Off to Siberia!*
We had to sit alone and listen,
suffering the steely gaze of other classmates
if we caused extra homework.

As a senior, I sat in another history class
when Mr. Dobson entered, his face as somber
as someone sharing news a friend or relative had died.
He whispered to our teacher both Twin Towers collapsed.
That year, some students readied to enlist;
others completed college apps.
Mr. Dobson sent me to mazes of books
when I asked about Iraq, Afghanistan, Palestine,
names I noticed scroll across the screen on network news,
countries I knew he covered in lessons I slept through.
That year, we learned of color-coded terror threat levels,
mailed anthrax attacks, but Mr. Dobson remained the same,
dressed in reliable blue khakis,
button-down shirts with pens poking out of pockets,
his office door always open to me
when I had pages marked and questions ready
like the eager student I never was.

Hunting Season

The way the rain pulls down leaves
reminds me of those long car rides
through Susquehanna County after school,
the foliage an explosion of orange and yellow
at October's end, when I slouched in the seat,
said little, and listened to the wiper blades
squeak against the windshield of my father's Ford.
October orange reminded me of his hunting suit,
what I didn't have in common with him—
the drive to wake up those cool autumn mornings,
lace up boots, polish a rifle, and then sit in a stand
and wait, attentive to the sound of twigs snapping
and possible game approaching.
He never asked me to follow into the woods,
but I indicated I wasn't interested
by locking my bedroom door, zoning out on video games.
I sat silent every day he picked me up,
leaned over the steering wheel,
and then leaned back and sighed
when I said little about my day.
The way the rain pulls down leaves still reminds me
of my father, his orange hunting suit hanging in the closet,
those autumn mornings he rose and knocked on my bedroom door,
how he wanted me to follow him, how I gave no reply.

Shifts at the Dollar Tree

At sixteen, I worked at the Dollar Tree,
buttoned up Polos to hide frayed
Clash and Dead Kennedys t-shirts,
what I wore on weekends at Café Roach,
where slam pits swelled and tattooed bodies
crashed against each other
until they dripped with sweat and stunk of booze.

At sixteen, I assured customers,
Yes, that really costs a dollar,
and on breaks thieved Pepsis and Snickers
while Randy the manager was locked
in his office, counting time sheets,
counting years he's been there.

At sixteen, I scribbled anti-capitalist
manifestos while Randy sat on boxes
in the stock room and told me,
Don't end up here forever, kid,
waving his hand in the air the way my dad did
whenever he wanted to make a point,
and when I looked up, I saw how Randy's hair receded,
how he squinted to read labels, even with glasses,

how he frequently rubbed his shoulders and back
the way my dad did after work,
how he had drum sticks tattooed on his left wrist,
but never spoke of his band, just that he jammed
in high school. He must have gone to places like Café Roach,
and maybe pounded the snare in a band, reliving such days
every time he air drummed in his office or the break room,
thinking no one was watching.

29

Picture of You in the '75 Corvette

When you died, cousin Gale gave me
the only picture of you she had
snapped when you just hit fifty,
your head turned towards the camera,
eyes hidden behind big black shades,
hair thinning, parted neatly, still more pepper than salt,
gold watch glistening on your wrist as your arm rested
on the driver's side door of the silver '75 Corvette.

You used to cruise through neighborhoods
in that car and crank Elvis cassettes,
to feel the King's cool, the King's youth,
and none of us knew cancer would come
a decade later, reduce you to hospital patient
thin, bony arms, bony legs,
mast tape holding tubes to your nose,
your canned food stacked on counters
like cat food. When that photo was taken,
I wanted a chance to hold the wheel,
to slouch in the driver's seat in a relaxed cool,
like James Dean in *Rebel Without a Cause*,
and learn how a sports car makes a man
feel younger, before all the cells go bad,
before the keys are turned over permanently,
before the car rusts in a garage.

Country Girl

She lives along Route 6,
where fracking trucks and tractors rumble along
the only highway in and out of towns
named Noxen, Wyalusing, specks on maps,
a road that ascends the mountain to a point
where clouds and fog could swallow cars,
spit them out at the bottom of a hill.
At night, she plugs her ears with headphones,
ignores frogs croaking louder than car horns.

In summer, she roams Main Street,
where orange hunting suits and rusted antiques
hang from shop windows.
She moves to McDonald's when streetlights flicker on,
fishes for change to buy a soda,
her price to stay and talk to friends
just as bored by bucolic farmland and lookouts
where teens turn their car lights low,
slink in their seats, blow off another Bible study.

She collects college mail from Ithaca,
Boston, Syracuse, imagines crowded cafes, bus stops,
bustling hallways, students scurrying to class.
She plots how best to leave,
how to let her parents and town down easy,
like a broken-hearted, bad date,
how to avoid a life dressed in soiled clothes,
bobbing on a tractor with a busted seat.

Girls at the Dairy Queen

These girls claim post office steps,
creating an island of cool a block down
from the Dairy Queen, where the line snakes
around corners and cars this first day of spring.
These girls wear checkered skirts and frayed jeans,
rolled up to show off red and blue Chucks
with ex-boyfriends's names scratched out or scribbled over,
replaced by Black Flag and Ramones logos
sharpied on the white toe. These girls jab
ice cream with spoons yellow and green,
bright likes streaks coloring their hair.
These girls plan first tattoos,
eager to turn eighteen when they won't need
mama's signature to ink up their arms. These girls
plot escapes to Philly or Boston,
cities where they can slip to clubs, slam dance
with other purple-hair outcasts.
These girls roll their eyes, go home to touch up
their hair dye, to shred clothes with safety pins,
to spin records and preen themselves
to look a little more punk.

Café Roach's Final Set

After the bloody brawls and blissful kisses,
five dollar shows and power chord blasts,
Café Del Soul unplugs.
Chairs are hauled away, half naked,
dressed in shredded sheets of memory.
The stage is stripped
board by board by men who never knew
what it's like to sweat in a circle pit
as feedback howls from amps.
The neon counter surrenders the tip jar,
while the wooden door waits
for the bulldozer's t-rex jaws to gnaw away,
until the building is flattened like a cigarette butt
stomped on by a punk rocker's boot.

Post-Deployment

I never asked you what it was like over there
in Iraq, the war I knew only from CNN commentary,
casualties that were not black body bags on evening news,
but statistics, unfamiliar names and numbers that scrolled
across the bottom of TV screens.
When I saw you post-deployment,
downing shots at bars, I never asked
if you killed someone, or how it felt to hold
a rifle, if you ever had to contemplate
squeezing the trigger to save your life.

We never talked war, but pretended
we were still in high school, crammed in
my Nissan, on our way to Philly
to catch punk shows in crowded basements,
where we thrashed and sang anthems
against capitalism and the mad war machine.

Bearded and back from Iraq, you still
jumped into the pit, while I hung in back
and watched you do the floor punch dance
to let out whatever aggression remained,
to forget the pained wailing of those casualties,
ghosts the rest of us couldn't understand
and you couldn't talk about,
no matter how bad the haunting,
no matter how much you wanted to be fifteen again,
years before you enlisted to pay for college,
but even the feedback of guitars
wasn't enough to silence those ghosts.

956 Johler Ave.

It is not your house on Johler Ave.
with the kicked-in metal fence,
dog shit on cracked sidewalks,
garbage cans left in the streets
days after the truck made its rounds,

the busted pool in back,
mud holes and patches of dry grass,
the white Chevy beached curbside,
plates still unregistered after months.

It is not your house on Johler Ave,
blocks from Weston Field where you chased
fireflies that glowed like your father's cigarettes
when he took a puff on the porch
after a day of touching up paint

and still played catch in the front yard.
It is not your bedroom with the cracked window
where your father once waved a broom,
trying to banish a bird that entered through the attic.

This is no longer your house one bad owner away
from condemned notices stapled to the front door,
do not enter tape waving like streamers,
the house with paint you thought would never flake and peel,
the neighborhood you're just passing through.

Rooftop Readings

Spring nights we drove to WEJL's
radio tower in downtown Scranton,
its red lights blinking like Christmas trees
or lighthouses calling ships home.

In back, we parked my battered Nissan,
jumped on the hood, swigged whiskey
until our chests burned,
and then hiked to the tower's rooftop.

Up there, you stomped your pink Doc Martins
in time with poetry
ripped from my high school journals,
written after shows at Café Roach,

where we met and you showed me
Emma Goldman books swiped from the library,
the first time I heard the word feminism
and learned about the anarchist activist arrested over birth control.

During rooftop readings, I watched your black
lipstick-traced lips read Goldman's manifestos
above a sea of city lights that glowed
like burning coal our grandfathers knew so well.

We never talked post-high school plans,
career paths like the rest of our friends.
You spoke of freight trains, said,
We'll see Seattle, maybe Chicago, visit Goldman's grave.

I never told you I fretted low SAT scores,
that college was my escape
from our parents' jobs punching factory clocks,
or graying in call centers, dying nowhere but Scranton-bound.

Up there, I dreamed of locomotives rumbling on train tracks,
packing a bag, joining you, feeling what it's like
when winds rush through open boxcars
and fill our lungs with this country's great air.

Up there, I clung to pages, yellowed
from cigarettes you sometimes sparked,
until we descended the rooftop and I returned to books,
eager for admittance to anywhere but State or Scranton U.

Watching War from the Dorms

On TV the war boomed like fireworks,
exploded green over trembling homes,
thundered like canons over evacuated streets.

Even my roommate turned from his laptop,
while I pressed my palm to my mouth,
still and silent while war was reduced

to shaky camera angles, breaking blog posts.
We watched in our dorm and no one
pounded the door, demanding action.

Few of us had siblings or cousins there,
and I had one acquaintance enlisted,
last seen in high school.

That February and March, A18 headlines whispered,
Largest protests since 'Nam, and when photos of the maimed
and charred Humvees emerged on the web,

I too joined on streets of New York and DC,
bused to big cities with anti-war veterans,
who first fought LBJ and Nixon,

and then the Texan who leveled cities with drones,
bulldozed Baghdad with tanks. These activists knew
how hands numb, how feet throb after hours of marching,

how to keep warm in crowded cafes,
as names of first casualties rolled by
on TV screens like desert sand,

while in our dorms my roommate muted news but let stay
No Blood for Oil signs plastered on our door.

South Street, Philadelphia, Friday Night

Couples seeking weekend kink slip into sex shops
where mannequins in black fishnets and pink wigs
wave from windows. Outside, a pot-bellied man howls,
repent, repent, clenching a silver cross that gleams
like a sword. Not one customer burns with shame,
no matter how much the corner preacher spews,
This city is a den of sin!

Down the block, a man in a frayed Phillies cap
spouts at city police, calls them *constitution killers,*
as corrupt as the halls of Congress
for arresting his friend who flashed a boob.
A neck-tattooed cop leans against his car, cracks a smile
when a Temple student staggers across the street,
screams, *Yeah, fuck the police, bro.*

A woman in a black sleeveless dress
walks her puffed-up Pomeranian through the scene,
causing a waitress on smoke break to bark,
Damn, that dog's an ugly piece of fuzz.
When the pet owner passes Crash, Bang, Boom,
two punks in eighty dollar bondage pants and hair the color
of neon restaurant signs stare and sneer, *yuppie.*
Like the cops and sex shop workers,
the woman presses on with a scrappy swagger
learned from the city that raised her.

As the Church Bells Rang

I was there when it happened,
when my father cocked his head to the side,
gasped and spit up green bile,
after I circled his bed with my mother
and siblings to recite the "Our Father,"
a prayer I last spoke in Sunday school,
years before the cancer, when my father paid me
five dollars to hike up Providence Road and attend church
at Saint Vincent's, after I protested, *But you and Mom never go.*
He knew he could persuade me by opening
his cracked leather wallet, pulling out a crumbled bill
while Mom said, *Stop giving him money all the time.*

In that hospital room, Mom clenched her crucifix necklace
that gleamed like the altar bell the priest rang
when I was boy and tried not to fall asleep in pews.
In that hospital room, Aunt Joyce sprinkled holy water on my
father, his body bone-thin,
his last breaths long and labored,
his final words reduced to moans the day before,
when I clenched his hand and said,
I promise I'll make it. It's okay to let go,
while Mom watched from a corner chair,
her hand on her forehead, though she couldn't believe
my father would not live to see me graduate,
or read my first byline,
or congratulate me on buying a home.
In that hospital room, while church bells chimed
at Saturday mass somewhere,
we hushed when father passed,
our heads bowed, our prayer done.

At Exit 170, I-81, I Blast the Ramones

This Saturday in February, I grip the wheel,
until my fingernails dig into my palms,
and I think of you that January night,
how your car spun out on I-81,
how newspapers said your body
catapulted through the windshield
and cars thumped over it.

As my wipers brush off slop and salt,
I blast *Rocket to Russia* and remember
that black Ramones shirt you wore
last time I saw you at the Bog, weeks before your death,
how Johnny, Dee Dee, Johnny and Marky's names
faded to peeling letters on cotton

and how you always said,
Too bad we weren't teens in '77
to catch them at CBGB's.

This Saturday in February my car crawls below 40,
slower near your exit as I crank the Ramones
to drown out the rumble of eighteen-wheelers, the roar of plows,
to forget how the buzz of my cellphone and news of your death
jolted me from sleep like a blaring car horn.

What I Kept in the Trunk of My First Car

In the trunk of my '92 Nissan,
I kept your military coat,
until it stunk of dust and grease.
When I cleaned out the car to sell for scrap,
I ran my hands along the sleeves,
remembering how the cuffs touched your small wrists,
adorned with black jelly bracelets.
I stared at the breast pockets, the cigarette burns
small brown circles. I recalled how you hid
packs of smokes, waited until I wasn't looking
to take puffs in the alley behind Metro,
our weekend hangout to catch punk shows.
On the coldest nights, when we shivered in my car,
and watched our breath rise in the air
like smoke rings from rustbelt factories,
I slid my hands under your coat and hugged you,
as we waited for the car to warm and cursed the heater
for spitting cool air. Other nights, I joked,
You look like a dude in that coat,
and you punched my arm,
until my skin bruised and swelled.
The summer night I pulled over to the side of the road
and said, *It's over. I'm getting out of this town,*
I waited for you to dig your nails into my arm
or punch me in the gut. Instead, you sat there,
leaned back in the seat, bit your bottom lip,
slipped off your coat.

Waiting for the Dead to Speak

Mother, I think of you widowed for ten years,
the way you slouched in the hospital chair
the day before father died, as I leaned over his bed,
squeezed his hand, and listened for any speech, any moan,
a sign he could hear what I said.

Mother, I think of the way you raised your palm
to your cheek and just listened
because you already said goodbye,
spoke final confessions, and waited
for the hour of passing.

I think of you now, the way you doze
on the leather recliner, the TV blaring local news
over and over, your head cocked to the side,
and I wonder if you dream of his face,
the stubble dotting his long jawline,
his brown eyes pleading for the chance
to speak again without a parched tongue,
without the slowed speech of someone who suffered a stroke.

I remember when you said you had a vision
of seeing him, and woke and still saw his face
inches from yours, one of those times you floated
in and out of consciousness, while flames danced
in the marble fireplace in a countryside home
you built together.

Mother, I want to ask how many times
you've seen his face. Was it gaunt and gray
like the hour of passing, or were his cheeks
tan and full like the father I remember?
How many times did you kneel at Sunday mass
and offer a prayer you were certain he'd hear?

I want to ask what you do
to call him forth because I haven't said his name
or visited his grave in ten years. I've had no visions,
and I remember how you said
the worst thing to do is to forget.

Mother, I want to remember how he looked
before his pained walk and palms full of cancer pills,
before he joked about his limp arm and inability
to hold a rifle and hunt. Mother, I remember you
in the hospital chair, and me leaning over his bed
saying what I had left to say because I never believed
the dead could hear us speak.

II

Seaside Summers

Morning. I gaze out my window at a gray mass—
fourth day without sunlight.
Restless, I rise from bed, read the news—
Sandy leaves thousands without power in Jersey.

I scroll through pictures of snaking gas lines,
gutted boardwalk, toppled rollercoasters.
I remember Seaside summers, when I clenched
my mom's hand through hordes of beachgoers.

I waited in line while coaster cars rattled wooden track,
and then jerked me around dips and bends.
At the top, before the first fifty-mile-per-hour free fall,
I gazed at the Atlantic cracking against sand.

Before the plunge, I closed my eyes, seized the bar,
though clinging to what remained of summer,
before packing for PA, before autumn
crept in like storm clouds.

I return to pictures of submerged cars,
buckled pavement, wind-ravaged homes,
hundreds standing in line, carrying red gasoline cans
under a moody November sky.

State of Emergency

Midnight. Streetlights blaze
like headlights slicing dark. Flakes fall
to suicide destinations, inches by the hour,
two feet by dawn. Boston is hushed,
Freedom Trail tracks erased,
sixteenth century graves encased in white,
Copley Square as still as farmland
before a storm, when animals cower
in barns, behind doors bolted against heaving winds.
This is normal now, neighborhood blackouts,
downed power lines spewing sparks like Roman candles,
ambulances squeezing down side streets, taxis idling
in garages. This is normal now, shorter gaps before the next
state of emergency, the next storm of the century.

Living with War

I remember students in hallways screaming,
Nuke the bastards, Nuke the bastards
after the president announced smart bombs
and ground troops in Afghanistan.
I remember when my classmate Lee
repeated the words *rag head, rag head*
over and over in art class, while I stood there,
drawing circles on the page, smoke billowing
from a building. I was too timid to stand up
and say, *Enough, asshole.*
I didn't want to be called a terrorist sympathizer.
I did march in New York and DC
against a second Iraq war, but knew
people chanting, *Not in our name*
would not be enough to halt war.
I still heard the phrases *rag head*
and *bomb them all* spew from counter-protestors,
waving American flags, revving their Harleys.
I knew how poll numbers reflected
their fever pitch and take 'em out attitude.
Now, over a decade later, my students whisper in class
about the latest images they've seen—
American journalists and a British aid worker
dressed in bright jump suits,
moments before the beheadings.
They slowly raise their hands when I ask
how many of them favor airstrikes in Iraq and Syria.
When I ask if they support ground troops,
a few fidget in their seats while they imagine
brothers, sisters, cousins, or friends doing another tour
in the Middle East. Their silence breaks when a student
in back says, *We know nothing else.*
We've always been at war.

August in Ferguson

Morning in mid-August and an American town smolders.
The newspapers reveal a teen's autopsy:
bullets in his arm, a bullet above his brow,
a bullet in his forehead.
By midnight in mid-August, a Missouri town burns.
Sound cannons blare,
while cops clench riot shields and confront
protestors masked in black bandanas.

SWAT-armored Humvees plow through streets,
guns pointed a few inches from protestors,
who raise their hands,
and cry out, *Hands up, don't shoot!*

Cops cuff reporters,
slam them into soda fountains,
smack their cameras down,
pound their bodies with rubber bullets and tear gas.

By Mid-August, videos replay Mike Brown's death.
Police refuse to release the officer's name, while his mother begs,
Justice for my son. Justice for my son, and protestors ask,
What country is this? What country is this?

The Doomsday Clock Reads 11:57

On the news, scientists warn we're closer to doomsday,
and move the atomic clock's hands
three minutes to midnight,
citing potential for nuclear and climate catastrophe.
In class, a student slouches in his seat,
pulls the drawstrings to his hoodie and whines,
I'm sick of this snow shit in April.
Whatever happened to global warming?
When I try to explain how climate change
disrupts normal weather patterns,
pushes polar vortex weather south,
he rolls his eyes, fidgets in his seat,
while another student asks,
What's the lesson all about today, teach?
I think of that doomsday clock,
three minutes to midnight, and I want to wave
my hands in the air, shout, *Listen, listen,*
Drive less. Recycle. Donate to polar bear funds.

Instead, we launch into peer editing workshops,
and I walk around the room, no longer vocal
about the climate change crisis because how do I show
melting ice caps or rising sea levels?
How do I explain that an inch of snow in April
doesn't mean climate change isn't real?
One student turns to another, asks,
Did this really happen? Hurricane Sandy left you homeless?
The author shifts in her seat and nods, and then
we have evidence, penned in a narrative, real enough
that students crane their necks, try to eye a line
from her paper, to learn what it means when nature
is mighty enough to swallow cars, pound shores,
and leave a student they know homeless,
while atomic scientists warn
we're three minutes from midnight.

The Poet's City

The green, graffitied sign tells me
I'm in Paterson, birthplace of Ginsberg,
five-book poem by Williams.
I ponder their quest to capture
new rhythms, an American idiom,
and wonder what they'd write about the city now—
the crossdresser on the corner,
her pink wig a contrast to slop and slush
on sidewalks, and dust and grime
of boarded-up storefronts.
Against February winds, she wears
a red leather skirt, torn fishnets,
stiletto heels that crunch ice,
while black men laugh and fist-bump
in front of pawn shops, as a mother
waddles across the street, her arms weighed down
by grocery bags while her children follow behind
and drivers blare their horns.
I think of Williams's poem "Proletariat Portrait,"
and the woman in it who pauses, pulls
a nail from her shoe, and then presses on,
like the crossdresser who touches up her lipstick,
and then moves forward on green,
the swagger of her hips a declaration
that this, too, is America.

On the Passing of Philip Levine

Phil Levine died four and a half years
after Occupy claimed Zuccotti Park,
before the NYPD swept in,
cuffed and detained, shoved bodies with batons.
For months, protestors demanded
a fair wage for the single mom working at Walmart,
relief for college students crushed by debt,
help for Detroit auto workers whose pensions
were raided and thieved before the crash,
workers with dusty faces,
the men and women of Levine's poetry.
That year, he ascended to poet laureate,
2011, the year of Occupy,
of activists shutting down the Brooklyn Bridge,
staging die-ins in DC parks,
setting up makeshift libraries in major cities.
That year, the country's poet,
tall and wiry, clenched podiums,
while outside government buildings and academic halls,
activists cried, *We are the ninety-nine percent,*
their bodies handcuffed and dragged off,
but not before two dozen more tents popped up,
while the country's poet leaned into the mic,
offered praise songs about what work is.

Thanksgiving, After the Riots

This Thanksgiving, an American town smolders,
while Target opens at 6 a.m.
and consumers crowd big screen TVs,
blaring and flashing throughout the store,
replaying images of Ferguson—
rows of businesses blackened,
charred like bombed-out buildings in Baghdad,
glass shattered across sidewalks,
sound cannons and tear gas fired upon protestors.
This Thanksgiving, the Brown family sets one less plate,
while a police officer preps for another prime time interview
to clear his name and declare
the teenager he killed looked like a demon,
ran through bullets, had Hulk-like strength.
This Thanksgiving, outraged activists tweet
#stop the parade, but pilgrim floats and Thomas the Tank
still loom over city streets, and marching bands still drum
and twirl batons, and families still slice turkey,
say grace, and clink wine glasses.
This Thanksgiving, the Brown family sets one less plate,
while children paint peace doves on boarded-up businesses
days after no indictment.

Taking the Pontiac to the Shop

after Stuart Kestenbaum

After six Scranton winters, 200,000 miles,
I take the Pontiac to the shop,
its rusted underbelly exposed on the lift,

mechanics shaking their heads like doctors
discovering a cancerous mass.
Inside: a record of my commute,

adjunct days zipping from school to school,
Doritos bags and Dunkin' Donuts cups littered
across the back, coffee stains on seats,

four different parking tags shoved
in the glove compartment, unclaimed student papers
stuffed under seats.

After three hours, a bill near
a grand, I pick her up,
surprised she no longer spits

cold air, or numbs my hands on the wheel.
I keep her for taking me somewhere stable,
a permanent employment tag hanging in the rearview.

Foreclosed Home

Hooks still hang in the attic
where the husband pounded the punching bag
every day after work, every day his site boss said,
I'll pay yah next week. Promise.

Black thumbprints still stain the wall,
near the hole the husband made
after the wife said,
Real men bring home bigger paychecks.

The furnished cabinet still sits in the kitchen,
coated with a landscape of dust,
left there since the wife ripped it out
after she shredded the foreclosure notice.

Tinkerbell stickers still plaster windows
in a blue room where a little girl
pressed pillows to her ears to muffle stomps and shouts
and dreamed of her family finding a new home.

Now another couple passes through, takes a card,
says, *We'll think about it,* while the realtor dims the lights,
locks the doors as streetlamps flicker over the For Sale sign.

Adjunct Plight

We work for cheap, settle easily.
Like road workers or factory hands,
we stand all day, shifting from foot to foot
to stay awake, and then crash on the couch,
a cold beer pressed to our lips,
dollar menu McNuggets for dinner.

We work for cheap, settle easily.
Like undocumented workers, we make less
than minimum wage, take what we can get,
keep what we have by hushing up.
We, too, are a booming statistic, but our names
unknown to full-time faculty and deans.

We work for cheap, settle easily.
Like our students, we too believed in loan debt,
that part-time gigs would not be permanent.
We migrate to different schools, different jobs,
leaving the classroom for the next adjunct
willing to work for cheap, settle easily.

At Thanksgiving Dinner

My crazy uncle tells me the president's a socialist,
a Muslim who wants to strip every federal courthouse
of Ten Commandment plaques and declare Sharia Law.
Clumps of mashed potatoes in his mouth,
he adds that Oprah hates white people and the way Barack
fist bumped Michelle on Election Night
was code for their plan to socialize healthcare.

When I tell him Obamacare is a rehash
of the GOP's plan from the 90s,
or explain how class inequality
is the worst since the 1920s
and Occupy Wall Street protests
aren't big union schemes to swell the welfare state,
he shoves a muffin in his mouth and barks,
Yeah, but the president wants to take away our guns,

and when he mentions Trayvon Martin,
how the jury was right to declare
George Zimmerman not guilty of murder,
I want to leap across the table,
yank on his tie, shove his face
in gobs of mashed potatoes and turnips,
but instead I lean back in my chair,
clench the arms white-knuckled
because even this crazy uncle is still family
and this is still Thanksgiving, and the way my mom's gaze
darts across the table reminds me to keep cool, to lean back,
to listen like a senator from a more civilized time,
willing to acknowledge and then refute the other side.

What I Found in Music

The day Joe Strummer died,
I locked my bedroom door,
played his discography,
starting with the Clash's debut,
ending with The Mescaleros.
I put on my *London Calling* shirt, washer-worn,
tattered with holes, and read his obit
again and again.

The day Joe Strummer died,
I remembered the first time I heard
"Clash City Rockers," how the track thundered
from my speakers, its charging chords
and Strummer's snarled lyrics a wake-up call.

I imagined him as a young front man in England,
part of the working-class that rose up,
demanded fairer wages, before becoming
the star who rocked Shea Stadium
beneath billboards for Coca-Cola, but still
released albums named after the Sandinistas.

The day Joe Strummer died, we were months
into the second Iraq war, and had no large protest movement,
no one like Joe to get up on stage and declare what's right
before blasting the audience with three-chord songs.

A decade after his death, we had Occupy Wall Street,
a movement with no leader, no organization, no soundtrack,
no one like Joe to ask, are you taking orders or are you taking over?
after Mayor Bloomberg swept away tent cities
and kicked out protestors with a few police orders.

Listening to Springsteen on I-81

The singer on the radio is Bruce Springsteen
belting out "The Ghost of Tom Joad,"
with Tom Morello filling in on guitar,
his fret board riffs as piercing as the Boss's vocals.

Hearing Bruce sing about shelter lines and a new world order,
I think of 80s pop icon Bruce with the boyish face,
the *Born in the USA* album, his ass on the cover
against the American Flag, the "Dancing in the Dark" video
played over and over on MTV, a pop hit still picked
during karaoke nights in my Scranton hometown.

I like this Bruce more, the one on the radio now,
who stood up to Reagan when he used
"Born in the U.S.A." as a campaign song,
ignoring its lyrics about a mistreated Vietnam vet.
I like this Bruce, who pays tribute to Steinbeck,
who spits political lyrics like a 1970s punk singer.

This singer on the radio makes me sympathize
with families sleeping in their cars
and makes me believe I saw the ghost of Tom Joad
when I pitched tents with protestors
in Philly's financial district, marched through streets,
waved cardboard signs about economic inequality.

This singer on the radio makes me forget his cheesy pop hits
and bad music videos, but remember Preacher Casey quoting Christ
about the last being first and the first being last,
as I pull off at a Scranton exit where another business
has fled the downtown, the mall has entered foreclosure
and the shelter lines swell.

Adjunct Blues

My dinged-up Honda sputters
to the next school, next class—
Freshman Comp 101, where students in sweats
yawn away my 8 a.m. lecture and the new recruit quarterback
slouches at his seat, texts while his girlfriend slides
her heels up his legs, tap, tap, tapping her pencil all class.

My dinged-up Honda sputters
to the next school, next office,
where the copier beeps and jams and I imagine
yanking out its wired guts, spilling coffee on its circuits,
clapping as it smokes and steams.

My dinged-up Honda sputters
to the next school, next community clinic
for a free flu shot and medicine to ease
my chronic cough. The secretary eyes my ironed
thrift store suit and tie, says, *You sure
you need this service?*

My dinged-up Honda sputters
to the next school, next class,
where I ghost through hallways, a blur
to full-time faculty. This time I leave
all lights on after 10 p.m., go home to red ink
my last stack of exams.

Writing the Last Word

A husband takes two bullets to the chest,
dies two hours after life flight.
Your editor says, *Snap a few photos.*
Coatesville homicides are old news,
unless you find someone decent to talk to.

At the scene, crimson drops on cracked sidewalks
blaze like carnival lights, calling neighbors and shrieking sirens
to the yellow-taped porch,
like a scene from a TV horror movie
where police trace chalk lines and answer few questions.

You fish for witnesses, find family
crammed in a one-floor, two-bedroom home,
the wife wailing, *They killed Sonny. They killed Sonny.*
She shoves a photo in your hand—
Sonny with a revolver-black goatee, wide grin, spaghetti-splashed apron

You don't ask why he was shot before
four months ago, if he pushed drugs.
You write he was a family man, community man,
whatever his wife says because you know
this will be the last time his name appears in print.

Temp Worker

He shakes his ass at Gateway Plaza,
the tax company's designated jester, dressed
in wrinkled Lady Liberty robes, a crown of foam spikes
flapping in raw January weather. Drivers blow by,
while he head bangs, fist pumps,
anything to catch their attention,
to earn commission, to keep a job.
He waves the plastic torch like a light saber near offices
where men in loafers and women in business skirts
sit high in heated spaces, while biting winds whip his skin,
numb his cheeks. Teenage boys fling assaults
from dinged-up first cars, howling,
Nice moves, queer. He keeps disco dancing,
pretending flickering streetlamps are club lights,
until his hands and ears warm, until April
pushes up flowers, until the next job—
summer long labor stocking shelves and pushing mops.

American Signs

Even in Quebec Province I couldn't escape
the Starbucks mermaid, her emerald crown
on sign after sign to Montreal's botanical gardens,
where I waited and sweat in July heat
to swipe my Visa and access the Chinese garden,
the aquatic garden, the insectarium,
where I overheard a teen declare
a green tea latte is boss,
but a cherry slushy from the 7/11 even better.

Later, when I wandered Quebec's cobblestone streets,
I saw the Starbucks S, sharp as dollar signs,
carved into stone buildings, near golden arches,
where tourists gobbled French fries, and then roamed
the Citadel, or snapped iPhone photos
near the St. Lawrence, white coffee cups in hand.
Crossing the border, I saw mermaids again,
hidden among Vermont's pointed Adirondacks,
their lips upturned in a smirk, though certain

I'd stop for something sweet,
something to spike the blood sugar,
something to burn my tongue, something familiar.

III

Before the Move

The day we moved into the home,
your mom spotted a plastic Saint Francis
perched on the kitchen windowsill.
She clenched the figurine and said,
See, see, this is a sign.
I told you this place was right.

Weeks before the move, before we inked form after form,
before we knew the history or read the deed,
I thought about the Smurl House two townships over,
the haunting that made national headlines,
the father's claim of a dead rat stink within walls,
how a chandelier crashed on the dining table,
inches from his daughter's head,
how the TV blared static like those scenes in *Poltergeist,*
how the wife levitated late at night and Stephen King
staked out the spookhouse for weeks, hoping
for a glimpse of the paranormal,
something for his next novel.

Weeks before we packed boxes, I thought of how little
we knew about the house, guessing its year
by the 1885 stamped on the claw foot bathtub.
We didn't know who lived there
before the last owners, or for how long,
if anyone died, if the walls creaked,
if the basement had a stink,
if anyone ever reported a haunting.

We got used to late night sounds,
the whoosh of heat blowing through vents,
the rumbling of pipes, icicles loosening,
smashing onto sidewalk, and in time, you said,
I *knew this place had good vibes,*
good energy. Months later, Saint Francis
still watches us from the windowsill.

Trying to Catch the Culprits

When we see a swastika graffitied on the red door
to the grounds-keeping building of Reese Park,
the paint silver and glaring like a knife blade,
you storm forward, ready to hunt and catch
whomever spray-painted the mark
a few feet from jungle gyms and swing sets,
the concrete area where kids dash
through fountains in summer.

Feet from our backyard, you search for cars
parked in the alley, headlights turned low,
the hangout where teens spark joints and toss trash
in our hedges. I want to grip your arm,
hold you back, as your fists hang heavy
at your sides and you ask,
Who the fuck did this?
I know you want to find and drag
the criminal through the streets,
or yank the teens out of their car
before your consider calling the cops,
like the time you ran down block after bock
in our old neighborhood, after someone stole your bike.
I knew you would knock the thief
to the ground, pummel them no matter their age.

We never found the bike,
and when we don't discover who vandalized the park,
I think of the lone Jewish family on Hoyt Street,
a few houses down, the way Bear and Rivka
hold their children's hands on the walk
to the synagogue each Saturday,
how they gave us garden vegetables last summer,
how their children play in that park with the boy McKale
across the street. When you ask, *What can we do?*
Should we spray-paint over it? I drive to Lowe's
and pay for the can to cover up another's crime,
before kids eye the symbol and ask what it means.

At the Front Door

I am always afraid you will show up at my doorstep,
demanding to know why I haven't called or texted,
why I accepted your Facebook request,
but never wrote on your wall or liked your status updates.
I am always afraid you will show up at my doorstep,
your hands still tightened to fists, ready to brawl
because of the time I threw you out of the apartment
after you said, *Go on hit me, College Boy*,
while your breath reaked of Coke and whiskey.
I am always afraid that you will forgive me
and want to hang at the Bog again,
until you down enough shots and slur enough pick-up lines
that I have to drive you home, like all those times I did
after I returned from college and found you
working at collection agencies, where you counted commission
and sold pot on the side to pay rent.
I am always afraid you will show up at my doorstep
and ask where I've gone, why I no longer call the old crew,
or drink Jack Daniels until I puke,
why I moved out of Scranton, into the 'burbs,
why I got engaged when the activist I used to be
always said, *Marriage is part of the fascist patriarchy*.
I am always afraid you will show up at my doorstep
and show me how personal politics and ideals change,
that you now zip around town in a BMW
and no longer spit and snarl at bankers, but have moved on
to hustling more expensive drugs or managing
collection agencies, circling the floors in a suit and polished shoes,
your barks and commands like the snap of a whip
causing workers in cubicles to dial faster
and not hang up until the other end pays up.
I am always afraid you will show up at my doorstep
and confess that you've burned the Chomsky books
and no longer protest the mad money oligarch
because after years of working doubles,
you're just too drunk or too tired to care.

Late Nights at Tom's Diner

I return to that photo of me
slouched in a red booth, eighteen,
college freshman at Tom's Diner, dressed
in a black hoodie plastered with punk pins—
Dead Boys, the Damned, the Clash,
groups disbanded before my birth.

My friend Stef leans on me
like a girlfriend, her hair wallpaper yellow
as I chug ice tea like beer, desperate
to turn twenty-one and slur punk rock
karaoke at Rex's, the town's lone dive bar.

We lingered at Tom's for second servings—
ninety-nine cent eggs, cold toast globed with jelly,
and then pogoed to The Dead Boys in our dorms,
until we passed out until afternoon class.

Stef moved across the country post-Ph.D.,
teaches Poli Sci at State now.
Attic dust coats my albums,
freed only when I need three-minute tracks
to blast me from reality—
mortgage, bills, pained longing for late nights
at Tom's, chats over Patti Smith's latest LP,
and pledges eighteen-year-olds make
to spin punk albums forever.

At Reese Park

July and from my window I see
kids dash through sprinklers at Reese Park,
their tan arms outstretched
in a game of tag.

Two teens hang in back,
sparking smokes they must have thieved
or paid someone to buy.
Markers in hand, they black and blue benches.

That evening, during our park stroll,
we discover their graffiti—
Fuck the park.
I got laid last night.

Your hands tighten to fists,
and your crossed arms tell me
you would pummel the closest punk
holding a Sharpie.

After you march home, retrieve paints,
I watch under a flickering streetlamp
as you brush over penises and fucks,
and it is then I remember

why I love you, as acrylics
streak your clothes, color your hands,
even spot your hair.

Burying the Rabbit

First day of May and we dig,
planting lettuce, sunflowers, green beans
in soil rich and turned over from last season.

We do this until our hands blister,
until dirt cakes our palms,
until you stop and shriek near the garden box

at a baby rabbit, dead,
its eyes half closed, a shine to them
like the plastic eyes of stuffed animals.

I plead for you not to show me more,
but I do look at its matted fur,
its snapped neck.

Under the poplar tree, we dig a different hole,
one to bury the dead, and remember
our cat's chase two days ago,

how we hoped the rabbit escaped.
Now Dante stretches out in the sun,
purring to be pet as we bury his prey.

You pluck a daffodil to place on the rabbit's body,
before we find a rock to mark the grave and remember
what rests near new roots spreading beneath soil.

By the Banks of the Susquehanna

Come spring, we trudge through mud,
our shoes squawking along the banks of the Susquehanna,
until we slip to woods, pop open beers
like teens playing hooky. We drink
to the sun, to the scent of lilacs
pushing up from damp ground. When the sunset shades
the sky red-yellow, we picnic while dragonflies
hum around our heads like tiny motor planes.
We could sleep here, after we count constellations,
stretched out under Orion's belt,
unconcerned with tomorrow's nine to five.
We could sleep here, like teens that sneak out late night,
eager to wear shorter clothes, to kiss each other hard
as moonlight spills onto water. We could sleep here,
our bodies entwined under gnarled branches in bloom.

Hiking with the Boys

When I take my nephews hiking,
they march forward, waving swords,
throwing rock grenades,
smashing icicles, splintering bark.

They dare each other
to cross the frozen pond,
and Michael does, one foot first,
before he dashes across.

He receives no prize, no candy,
just a high five, enough to prove manhood,
to make his younger brother Josh
jump and yell, *Watch me, watch me.*

He too wants a chance to be like those superheroes
they watch each Saturday, Wolverine who heals
after rounds of bullets, Superman who punches through walls,
Batman who hog ties bad guys,

all of them saving the day and the damsel.
When Josh plunges a stick at his brother,
scraping his left cheek, for a moment
Michael's bottom lip quivers, and he turns

so we don't catch him wiping tears
on his hoodie, so his brother doesn't call him
sissy, wimp, coward, names meant to chip away
at his tough guy imitation of Saturday morning superheroes.

I, too, played good guy as a kid,
lined up plastic army men on shelves,
imagined myself dressed in fatigues, rifle-armed and ready
to crawl under barbed wire or snipe bad guys.

I, too, hid tears after accepting a foolish dare,
skateboarding across cracked sidewalk, crashing,
breaking my wrist, biting my lip to quell
sobs in front of friends, until home,

where boys can lock doors and cry
while brothers disarm and offer ice.

Home Ownership

What they don't teach you when you buy a house
is how to tend the existing garden, if the tulips
and irises will push up spring after spring,
if the cherry blossom tree has to be trimmed,
if you killed the hyacinths by cutting shriveled stems,
if the blueberry bushes will green come June,
if overgrown mint will strangle nearby flowers.

What they don't teach you when you buy a house
is when to lay down mulch, how many bags to buy,
why spots of your lawn are still brown in July,
if it's grubs or something worse.

What they don't teach you when you buy a house
is how to make the home look as good
as it did for the last owners,
the young couple who power washed the siding,
planted perennials, displayed flags for each season
and hanging baskets all spring and summer.

What they don't teach you when you buy a house
is how to start the leaf blower or shrub trimmer,
so the neighbors drinking beers on nearby porches
don't think you can't use power tools.

What they don't teach you when you buy a house
is where to place the art, where to store the books,
how to arrange the rooms and groom the garden,
so the new place feels like yours.

Praise Poem

This is not another poem about my father,
but for my mother, who still says,
Iron your shirt and tuck it in,
whenever I visit before work.

This is a poem for my mother,
who gave me ten dollars for my first book,
five dollars shy of the cover price, and said,
I birthed you. That's enough.

This is a poem for my mother,
who still eyes weekly bank statements
and saves and skimps, spends little on herself,
but always filled kitchen cupboards for five kids.

This is a poem for my mother,
who often fell asleep on the recliner
after my father died, her mouth open,
as though about to sigh.

This is a poem for my mother,
who learned how to gas up the John Deere,
how to cut branches, how to go on living in a house
she built with my father and refused to sell after he died.

I Imagine Gardening with My Father

Father, I think of you, dead ten years, and remember
how you rubbed your back and limped to the kitchen
after swinging the weed whacker back and forth,
or hunching over the hood of a car to change its oil.
I like to imagine you alive, visiting my home,
drinking a Coors on the patio, a Saturday afternoon,
one of those first warm days of spring.
I imagine you inspecting my yard, pointing at the garden box,
recommending when to plant tomatoes, when to lay mulch.
I imagine you visiting during summer months,
kneeling next to me in the yard.
I imagine us planting together, our hands dirty,
the calluses and cracks of your palms
evident, after years working at an army depot,
after years of doing yard work.
I don't imagine your temper, your flushed cheeks,
or the way you spit when you yelled. Instead, I imagine us together,
wiping sweat against the sleeves of our t-shirts,
as we dig and plant and forget
that your body no longer moves the way it used to,
that your son is old enough to own a home.
Father, I think of you, dead ten years, and remember
when I was a boy, how you scooped me in your arms,
lifted me above your head.
Now I imagine the sun warm against your cheeks,
your skin tan enough, your hair dark enough
to make you look like the father I remember.

Unwritten

First day of class he lumbers in,
hoodie yellow and orange like a lighter's flame,
flint of nicotine visible when he smiles.

When I ask about narratives, their stories,
he raises his hand, hospital wristband glistening.
Man, why we gotta get so personal?

First draft I read how he used to work doubles,
hustled filling French fry cups, and then scrubbed
so the fast food stink didn't follow to class.

Next draft I learn how he sipped whiskey
from slushy cups, until he vomited on a burger
and the boss barked, *You're fired.*

Three weeks later, his dad calls, says,
My son's all screwed up,
in rehab again. Can he still pass?

Like a nurse, I file his son's info and essay,
as though waiting for him to rise again,
transfigured, to finish the narrative, then sign himself out.

Raking Leaves

There is something soothing about the scrape of a rake,
the rhythmic process of pulling dead leaves,
bending to pick them up, dumping them
in curbside lawn bags,
something soothing about the way the sun
warms your hair one of these last
seventy-degree days as you labor past
soreness in your arms, until you forget
emails to send, reports to file,
take-home work you left at the office,
until you forget the splendid mums will shrivel,
the tree that sheds now will wear nothing soon,
and you will curse the cold.

Waiting Out the Storm

At the top of the Ferris wheel, we watched parents
clench their children's hands and dash
to park exits, while rain pounded tents
and workers huddled in ticket stands,
shivering in ponchos. Before the downpour,
I wanted to wait for the mass of gray to pass,
but you pulled my hand, tugged me
to the line, said, *Come on. It'll be fine.*
You never take risks.
You knew that I was afraid of heights,
and while rain hammered pavement, silenced rides,
I leaned closer, confessed, *I'm nauseous,*
while our car swung back and forth, back and forth.
At the first rumble of thunder,
I thought of all the ways we could die—
struck by lightning, crushed by a wind-snapped tree,
or worse, by plummeting to the ground if the ride's rusty bolts
shook loose and popped out one by one.
When they stopped the Ferris wheel, we waited
for passengers to exit and inched lower and lower,
closer to the ticket booth, to an exit.
At the top, you leaned in, said, *I'm sorry I made you do this.*
You pointed to the red glow of sunlight in the distance,
pushing through storm clouds, and then, I wanted to linger
because I felt like a hiker, who reached some great peak,
holding your hand, watching the day's sunrise,
until we jerked to a stop, and I seized your arm,
rushed to our car, where we scrunched our knees
against the dash, and waited for the rain to stop.

Sunset over the St. Lawrence

Our last night in Quebec,
we stay in St. Antoine de Tilly,
where farmland stretches and rolls,
green and lush these waning July days.

We pop blueberries into our mouths,
split a tomato given to us
by our host family, the juice and seeds
cool on our tongue, as the sun sets
over the St. Lawrence, a red thumbnail,
brighter than the glow of cigarettes smoked outside
Quebec City's cobblestone street cafes.

We step to the edge at low tide,
watch freights blink green and red,
as the yellow of nearby villages
reminds us of towns back home
lit against Pennsylvania Appalachians.

We linger and listen to leaves rustle,
the breeze a welcome cool down
before the merciless days of August
into autumn, when these trees will blaze
like the sunset over the St. Lawrence.

September

and I look at the lilies,
their petals about to fall
on remaining green,
while I wonder if it is my fault,
if I did not water them long enough,
if I did not lay enough mulch in May
to halt choking weeds.

September and I tend the garden,
where dill browns and bends in surrender
to cooler winds and waning sunlight,
while lettuce thins to green shoots,
and the last crown of broccoli
explodes to yellow flowers.

It is September and cherry tomatoes still ripen—
bright dots on green vines I pick,
before they split and wilt,
before they fall and I regret
not saving the season's remaining crops
before dry leaves drift across the backyard
and the wind sorts what to destroy.

Facing Late Autumn

The leaves lay like a wound,
red and deep across the lawn, while what remains
is frightened away by bursts of November wind.
I look at concrete-gray clouds and sigh,
knowing it is time to cover flower beds,
yank out roots of annuals,
their petals shriveled and frail, as fine as dust
released to the air.
Soon I will cut back roots of perennials,
until everything in the yard is brown,
until birds no longer chirp,
but vacate their nests,
more visible now as branches of trees
shake against the wind
and scrape against windows like angry fingers,
while the house creaks at its joints.

Wind Chimes

After my mother rips off wrapping paper,
removes bows from the box,
and unpacks the wind chimes,
I watch her tap the rods,
so the bells ring in a room crowded
with grandchildren clenching iPhones and iPads.
I wonder where she will hang them,
maybe from one of the unused hooks
on the porch, where my father
used to take slow drags of Marlboros.
The smoke coiled near his cheeks,
while he stared at patches of trees ahead,
his hands and frayed cut-off shorts
streaked with blue paint
after he touched up the banister.
I wonder if my mother will sit on the porch swing,
its paint flaked and chipped, and listen
to the wind blow through the grass
and sound the chimes.
Will she feel lonely?
For now, she says thank you for the present,
slips it back in the box,
at least until spring or summer
when she has to decide where to hang the chimes
on the porch my father used to occupy.

Rain on Christmas Eve

Christmas Eve, and I gaze out the window
at the cage of trees, the sparrows
hopping from branch to branch.
The clouds look like torn rags,
soiled, spitting rain all morning.
This weather is too warm for snow,
too warm for iced-up sidewalks,
too warm for puffs of breath.
Christmas Eve, I sit at the table, grateful
for the past year, the love of one
who still sleeps, cocooned in a blanket,
while rain hammers windows.
Christmas Eve, I gaze out the window, staring
at the Sunoco down the street, where drivers
bolt from their cars to the convenience store
for milk or eggs, whatever is still needed,
before they dash back to their cars
and drive off to their cozy homes,
while the sparrows find shelter in trees and sing,
no matter how heavy the rain.

Haircut

I closed my eyes, leaned against the wall,
a blue towel draped around my neck, as I trusted
your hands with scissors and listened to snips
near my ears, near my neck, chopping clumps
of black hair, grown into little wings and curls, you said.
I never flinched when you leaned in, close enough
to feel your breath upon my neck and the blades
grazing my earlobes. We said nothing
as you shaped my hair the way you wanted it
and paused to study your work, the way you paused
while working on a painting and thought of color and contrast,
tilting your head to the side, before another brushstroke.
I listened when you pressed the black comb
against my eyebrows and said, *Don't move now.*
I didn't wince at the electric buzzer,
even though I knew a nudge of your hand
could scratch my cornea.
During the final weeks, before the break-up,
when we knew one of us had to move out,
I took my place against the wall,
pulled a towel around my neck and trusted
that your hands would not slip.

Mid-Winter Scene

Today, the trees give nothing, naked
beneath a gray sky.
Today, my car inches over dirt roads,
as I slow down and eye fields of white
and ponder the dead—
my father, who laced up boots,
slipped on black gloves,
shoveled the sidewalk
in front of our countryside home.
A kid, I peered out the bedroom window,
spotted the green of his Packers jacket,
watched puffs of his breath rise as he hunched over.
I helped when I felt guilty.
Today, I think of the dead, grandfathers
I never met, and how their backs
must have bent like my father's
as they labored in mines,
stopping only to wipe sweat and breathe.
Today, I think of the home we owned
before I split, before the next guy moved in,
and how I, like my father,
shoveled as inches accumulated.
Today, I wonder if you or someone else
clear snow the way my father did,
the way I did until I saw concrete beneath white.
Today I ponder the dead, old ghosts,
bare trees in vast fields.

Late January Hike

Ice cracks beneath my boots,
as I recall our hikes together,
how you stopped on the trail, tilted
your head back, spread your arms,
as though to soar away like one of the hawks
we spotted above pines.
You closed your eyes, leaned
into sunlight and said,
Stay with me here a moment.
On this day, I pause
and feel the sun upon my cheeks,
its touch as relaxing as your fingers in my hair.
When I open my eyes, I see the hushed
trail before me and wonder
where you are now, what you are doing.
Did you lace up your boots and find a new path?
I remember what you pointed out to me on past hikes—
cardinal red in trees,
deer prints in fresh snow,
names of plants first to bloom after the thaw.
I remember how your gloved hand slipped into mine,
and now I stare at the quiet path before me,
my walk as solitary as the hawk I spot
hovering above barren trees.

Driving Along Countryside Roads, Mid-Winter, Pennsylvania

I slow my car and listen
to cinders and packed snow
crunch beneath my tires.
I stare at fields, miles of white,
naked branches of trees
shaking beneath a gray sky.
This is February,
mid-winter, Pennsylvania,
and I want you beside me,
your hand curled into mine,
while we spot a cardinal
in the distance, bright and red,
like Valentine's Day hearts
hanging in windows of countryside homes.
I want to open your door,
stand with you, kiss you,
and then watch puffs of your breath
rise and disappear into the gray.
This is February,
mid-winter, Pennsylvania,
and I want you beside me,
to inhale the cold and know
that we are alive,
as much as those trees in the distance,
alive as much as roots buried deep
beneath layers of ice and snow.
I want to kiss you, here,
on the roadside, near the fields,
while winds snap against our cheeks,
and the cardinal takes flight,
soars above us, a splash of red
beneath the gray, while I kiss you
long and hard, here, on the roadside,
February, mid-winter, Pennsylvania.

Surviving Winter

This winter almost killed me,
all those commutes down I-81,
clenching the wheel, white-knuckled,
sweating, while walls of snow flew off eighteen-wheelers,
and my Hyundai trudged through ice.

When I arrived at class, lectured
before half-empty rooms, I realized
how little it mattered if I covered MLA
or reviewed Imagism for Friday's quiz
because we all gazed out the window,

watched sleet slick up roads,
cars swerve out of lanes,
while we waited for a text to tell us
evening classes would be canceled.

Now it is April, and the sky threatens rain.
Students huddle in libraries to finish final papers,
and I sigh when I walk on sidewalks and see
streaks of color against gray—
red and yellow tulips, crocuses sprouting
like green fingers rising from Earth.

Never have I needed summer as I do now,
after all those mornings squinting
through an ice-streaked windshield,
all those afternoons stuck behind plow trucks,
inching towards home on I-81,
closer to the semester's end.

Remembering the Dead

I never visit the graves of relatives,
or trace my fingers over the dates
of when they were born, when they died.
I don't remember where I stood
at Cathedral Cemetery that February morning
we lowered my father's casket.
I don't remember if the cool
wind of mid-October touched my face
when we circled my grandmother's grave
and I shifted from foot to foot, unsure what to say.
I don't even visit the grave of my departed cat, Dante,
laid to rest on the side of the house,
a stone set on soil to mark the spot.
I choose to remember anisette cookies
my grandmother gave me for my birthday,
the sprinkles as bright as wrapping paper,
and how my aunts joked she withheld an ingredient
from the recipe she copied on index cards.
I choose to remember how my father
parked his black and red Ford
on the grassy lawn of Mountain View High
and beeped the horn when I couldn't spot him
all those days he picked me up after school.
I choose to remember the way Dante
jumped on to my writing desk,
nudged my hand and purred.

Awaiting the Thaw

Last day of March and flakes fall,
fat and heavy like snow that coated sidewalks
that January day when I shoved belongings
into my trunk and piled the rest on the backseat.

I lingered and stared at the 17 carved on red wood
near the mailbox, and remembered when we looked
at the house together two years earlier. Thunder cracked,
and rain pounded the outside patio. Still,

you pulled the drawstrings to your hoodie,
explored the backyard where your shoes sunk
into the damp yard as red and yellow tulips
contrasted the gray sky.

This could be ours, you said, pointing
to flowerbeds, where we would preen
hyacinths and hydrangeas that coming summer,
after the move and before the arguments.

The day I left, I stared at the 17, and recalled
how we huddled on the wraparound porch,
awaited the realtor, peeked through windows and pondered
what type of life and home could be ours.

Soon, April will come in like a lover,
her touch warm enough to disrobe March's white coat,
and I will bend low in a new backyard to prep a garden,
and lay new roots beneath fresh soil.

Lady Day Sings the Blues on YouTube

When I ask the class if they know Billie Holiday,
a few raise their hands, while others squint
at her name scrawled across the board,
as though trying to solve a math problem.

I pull up a YouTube video—
Billie black and white on TV,
sleek in a silk dress,
doing a slow sway on stage,
her voice not yet heroin-burned,
her eyes not yet blood drop red.

Where's the beats? a student asks,
hearing bursts of trumpet and sax.
Where's her dancers? another questions,
eyeing her backup band, still on stage,
except for their frantic finger motions
hitting notes on brass.

A full verse in, they hush,
until Lady Day's final note—
God bless the child who's got his own, got his own,
her face pained, pulled back until release.
Now they know what Langston meant
in "Song to Billie" by a muted trumpet,
a sorrow dusted with despair.

What Our Cat Teaches Me in Dreams

I follow our departed cat Dante
from room to room in the house we owned,
his house, too, with tufts of fur in the carpet.

We pause in the dining room,
where my writing desk used to be.
Each morning, you found us there,

as he stretched across streaks of sunlight
and nudged my arms, while you cupped your hands
around a coffee mug.

I want Dante to lead me to a room
where I'd find you sketching,
your gaze rising to find mine.

Instead, Dante paws at the back door,
where he escaped and then returned,
too weak to walk, ridges of spine visible.

In dreams, he's bright-eyed,
purrs to be pet. When I bend to comply,
I wake up and recall how he brushed my legs,

urged me to move forward, not linger
in rooms I used to call home.

While You Painted

I imagine you in college
sitting at some café, an indie band
crooning through speakers,
walls adorned with student paintings.
Your work would be there too,
and you must have studied it,
while sipping tea and pondering
different colors, a different focus.

I imagine your messenger bag sagging
with pounds of art history books,
tops of their spines frayed.
I imagine you on a date, leaning over the table,
listening to some boy who preached
revolution, waved his red I.W.W. card,
and said he'd risk arrest, join sit-down strikes.

Did he ever act or just talk?
I imagine that you listened and smiled
when his hand brushed yours,
as he looked for socialist meaning in your art
and asked if you ever heard of the Wobblies.

Now, I recall those first months
of our relationship, when you joined me
to occupy Boston's banking district
and crouched on pavement,
painted signs for protestors. When I dove
in the crowd, marched down streets, you lingered
in back, said nothing, expecting more than chants
about bad banksters and the ninety-nine percent.

You knew what that college date never knew,
what I never knew.
Slogans are just talk, like that college boy,
unwilling to act, to lean across that table and kiss you.
Slogans fade, like smeared ink on protest signs,
unlike your paintings, seen by those café regulars,
colors sustained and absorbed on canvas.

Learning to Garden

You think of her these first days of spring
and the tulips you planted behind the house,
orange and red, bright for a few weeks,
until they shrink to slender stems and their color
is given away to the wind.

The relationship was like that, never finite,
fragile enough to tear from one more gust,
one more outburst, one more argument,
and it too blazed at moments,
from the squeeze of her hand in the movie theater,

or the spark of a kiss during those art walk dates.
You think of her these first warm days
and wonder if she's pausing beneath the weeping willow
along the river walk. You remember she said its leaves
looked like a firework unfolding into night.

She taught you to call flowers by their right names,
and now you kneel in dirt because you learned
what it means to garden and when to lay the tarp
so what blooms can withstand
rare frost and sudden bursts of wind.

The New York Quarterly Foundation, Inc.
New York, New York

Poetry
Magazine

Since 1969

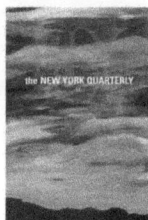

Edgy, fresh, groundbreaking, eclectic—voices from all walks of life.

Definitely NOT your mama's poetry magazine!

The *New York Quarterly* has been defining the term contemporary American poetry since its first craft interview with W. H. Auden.

Interviews • Essays • and of course, lots of poems.

www.nyq.org

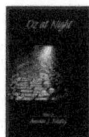

No contest! That's correct, NYQ Books are NO CONTEST to other small presses because we do not support ourselves through contests. Our books are carefully selected by invitation only, so you know that NYQ Books are produced with the same editorial integrity as the magazine that has brought you the most eclectic contemporary American poetry since 1969.

Books

www.nyq.org

poetry at the edge™

www.ingramcontent.com/pod-product-compliance
Lightning Source LLC
LaVergne TN
LVHW091227080426
835509LV00009B/1202